In This Catholic Church

By **Maura Roan McKeegan**

Illustrated by **Ted Schluenderfritz**

OSV Kids

Huntington, Indiana

In memory of Father Al Hewett (1924-2020), who lived his priesthood with a heart full of love and pure joy.

Maura Roan McKeegan

✠

For my mom, Suzanne Fritz
1941–2022

Ted Schluenderfritz

28 27 26 25 24 23   1 2 3 4 5 6 7 8 9

Our Sunday Visitor Publishing Division
Our Sunday Visitor, Inc.
200 Noll Plaza
Huntington, IN 46750
1-800-348-2440

ISBN: 978-1-68192-763-3 (Inventory No. T2631)
LCCN: 2022940745

Cover design: Lindsey Riesen
Cover art: Ted Schluenderfritz
Interior design: Lindsey Riesen
Interior art: Ted Schluenderfritz

Printed in the United States of America

"Open, open wide the doors to Christ!"

Pope St. John Paul II

Here is a door
That's open wide
For all God's children
To come inside.

And through this door,
There is a church,
A Catholic church
With its doors open wide
And God's children inside.

And in this church,
There is a boy,
An altar boy
In a Catholic church
With its doors open wide
And God's children inside.

And near that boy,
There is a candle,
A candle lit
By the altar boy
In a Catholic church
With its doors open wide
And God's children inside.

And watching that candle,
There is a child,
A darling child
Who likes the light
From the candle lit
By the altar boy
In a Catholic church
With its doors open wide
And God's children inside.

And with that child,
There is a mom,
A loving mom
Who holds the child,
The darling child
Who likes the light
From the candle lit
By the altar boy
In a Catholic church
With its doors open wide
And God's children inside.

And next to that mom,
There is a dad,
A faithful dad
Who sings all the hymns
With the loving mom
Who holds the child,
The darling child
Who likes the light
From the candle lit
By the altar boy
In a Catholic church
With its doors open wide
And God's children inside.

And close to that dad,
There is a girl,
A thoughtful girl
Who treasures the way
That her faithful dad
Sings all the hymns
With the loving mom
Who holds the child,
The darling child
Who likes the light
From the candle lit
By the altar boy
In a Catholic church
With its doors open wide
And God's children inside.

And behind that girl,
There is a sister,
A religious sister
Who quietly prays
For the thoughtful girl
Who treasures the way
That her faithful dad
Sings all the hymns
With the loving mom
Who holds the child,
The darling child
Who likes the light
From the candle lit
By the altar boy
In a Catholic church
With its doors open wide
And God's children inside.

And beside that sister,
There is a man,
A kind old man
Who kneels with his cane
By the religious sister
Who quietly prays
For the thoughtful girl
Who treasures the way
That her faithful dad
Sings all the hymns
With the loving mom
Who holds the child,
The darling child
Who likes the light
From the candle lit
By the altar boy
In a Catholic church
With its doors open wide
And God's children inside.

And at the altar,
There is a priest,
A joyful priest
Who offers the Mass,
While the kind old man
Kneels down with his cane
By the religious sister
Who quietly prays
For the thoughtful girl
Who treasures the way
That her faithful dad
Sings all the hymns
With the loving mom
Who holds the child,
The darling child
Who likes the light
From the candle lit
By the altar boy
In a Catholic church
With its doors open wide
And God's children inside.

And in the priest's hands,
There is a Host,
A Sacred Host,
Lifted up high
By the joyful priest
Who offers the Mass,
While the kind old man
Kneels down with his cane
By the religious sister
Who quietly prays
For the thoughtful girl
Who treasures the way
That her faithful dad
Sings all the hymns
With the loving mom
Who holds the child,
The darling child
Who likes the light
From the candle lit
By the altar boy
In a Catholic church
With its doors open wide
And God's children inside.

And here in this church
Is Jesus Christ,
Sharing his love
And giving new life
In the Sacred Host,
Lifted up high
By the joyful priest
Who offers the Mass,
While the kind old man
Kneels down with his cane
By the religious sister
Who quietly prays
For the thoughtful girl
Who treasures the way
That her faithful dad
Sings all the hymns
With the loving mom
Who holds the child,
The darling child
Who likes the light
From the candle lit
By the altar boy
In a Catholic church
With its doors open wide
And God's children inside.

Jesus Christ is the Sacred Host.

He abides in the hearts of His people.

Jesus Christ is the Light of the World.

And His love is alive in this Catholic Church.

Praised be Jesus Christ, now and forever!

OSV Kids

Helping families love and live the Catholic faith

OSV Kids is an exciting new brand on a mission to help children learn about, live, and love the Catholic Faith. Every OSV Kids product is prayerfully developed to introduce children of all ages to Jesus and his Church. Using beautiful artwork, engaging storytelling, and fun activities, OSV Kids products help families form and develop their Catholic identity and learn to live the faith with great joy.

OSV Kids is a monthly magazine that delivers a fun, trustworthy, and faith-filled set of stories, images, and activities designed to help Catholic families with children ages 2-6 build up their domestic churches and live the liturgical year at home.

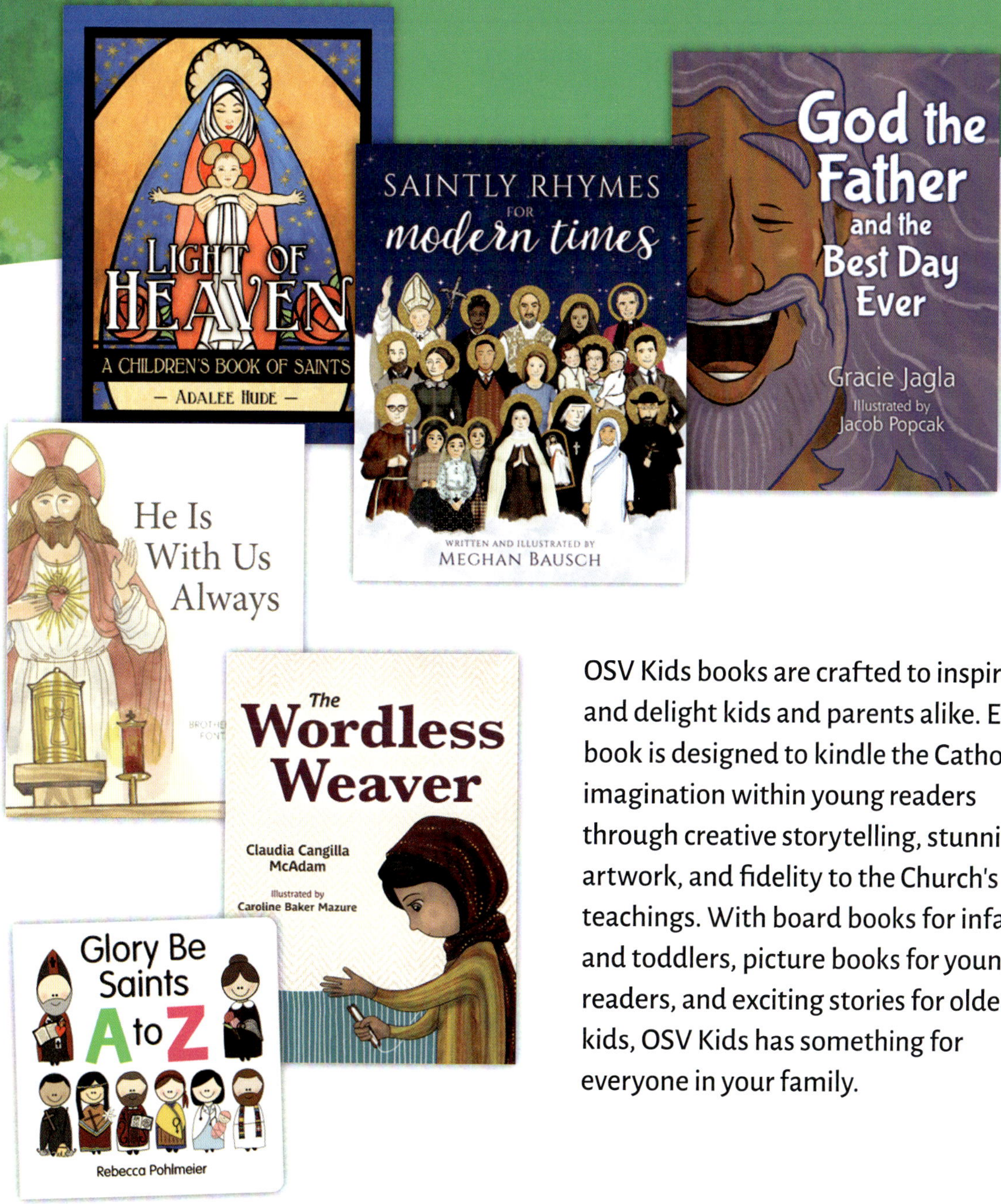
LIGHT OF HEAVEN
A CHILDREN'S BOOK OF SAINTS
— ADALEE HUDE —
SAINTLY RHYMES FOR modern times
WRITTEN AND ILLUSTRATED BY
MEGHAN BAUSCH
God the Father and the Best Day Ever
Gracie Jagla
Illustrated by
Jacob Popcak
He Is With Us Always
The Wordless Weaver
Claudia Cangilla McAdam
Illustrated by
Caroline Baker Mazure
Glory Be Saints A to Z
Rebecca Pohlmeier

About the Author

Maura Roan McKeegan is an award-winning author of a number of Catholic children's books, including *Into the Sea, Out of the Tomb: Jonah and Jesus*; *St. Conrad and the Wildfire*; *Where is Jesus Hidden?*; and *The Poorest Shepherd*. She also writes articles for various magazines. As a former classroom reading teacher, she has a passion for picture books. "I love the way picture books reach across generations to bring the joy and simplicity of childhood to readers of all ages, from the very young to the very old," she says. Reading aloud with children is her favorite hobby.

About the Illustrator

Ted Schluenderfritz has worked in the Catholic publishing world for the past twenty years as an illustrator and graphic designer. He has been the art director for magazines such as *Catholic Digest*, *Envoy*, and *Gilbert Magazine*. Besides editorial illustration, he has illustrated several children's books, including *Portrait of the Son* by Josephine Nobisso, the *Old and New* series by Maura Roan McKeegan, and *The Attic Saint* by Tim Drake. He and his family publish an online magazine for children and their parents, 5sparrows.com, which features original stories, liturgical reflections, puzzles, games, and much more. To see more of his art, visit him on Instagram @schluenderfritz and @5sparrowskids.